SPOTLIGHT ON EARTH SCIENCE

ISLANDS AND ARCHIPELAGOS

MICHAEL SALAKA

PowerKiDS press™

NEW YORK

Published in 2017 by The Rosen Publishing Group, Inc.
29 East 21st Street, New York, NY 10010

Editor: Melissa Raé Shofner
Book Design: Michael Flynn
Interior Layout: Mickey Harmon

Photo Credits: Cover (image) GARDEL Bertrand / hemis.fr/Getty Images; p. 5 Toshitaka Morita/Getty Images; p. 7 Walter Myers/Stocktrek Images/Getty Images; p. 8 Igor Plotnikov/Shutterstock.com; p. 9 Kanuman/Shutterstock.com; p. 10 Lukiyanova Natalia/frenta/Shutterstock.com; p. 11 Anton Balazh/Shutterstock.com; p. 13 https://upload.wikimedia.org/wikipedia/commons/4/49/Krakatoa_eruption_lithograph.jpg; p. 14 R McIntyre/Shutterstock.com; p. 15 https://upload.wikimedia.org/wikipedia/commons/c/c0/Long_Island_Landsat_Mosaic.jpg; p. 16 Mario Hagen/Shutterstock.com; p. 17 KARIM SAHIB/AFP/Getty Images; p. 19 Melinda Podor/Getty Images; p. 19 (inset) mavl/Shutterstock.com; p. 20 Pichugin Dmitry/Shutterstock.com; p. 21 Dmitri Korobtsov/Getty Images; p. 22 Todd Hackwelder/Shutterstock.com.

Cataloging-In-Publication Data

Names: Salaka, Michael.
Title: Islands and archipelagos / Michael Salaka.
Description: New York : PowerKids Press, 2017. | Series: Spotlight on earth science | Includes index.
Identifiers: ISBN 9781499425178 (pbk.) | ISBN 9781499425208 (library bound) | ISBN 9781499425185 (6 pack)
Subjects: LCSH: Islands--Juvenile literature.
Classification: LCC GB471.S25 2017 | DDC 551.42--d23

Manufactured in China

CPSIA Compliance Information: Batch #BW17PK For further information contact Rosen Publishing, New York, New York at 1-800-237-9932.

CONTENTS

CHAPTER ONE

SURROUNDED BY WATER

An island is an area of land surrounded by water on all sides. Islands are found all over the world in lakes, oceans, and even rivers. The main types of islands are continental and oceanic, but other types also exist.

Islands come in all shapes and sizes, and many different kinds of plants and animals live on them. Some islands have a cold climate and are covered in ice year round, while others have a very hot climate. Sometimes an island will be isolated, or very far from the nearest continent or other islands. The plants and animals living on these isolated islands can be very unusual.

Not all islands are isolated. In fact, sometimes islands are located close to each other in groups. These groups are called archipelagos. Hawaii and Japan are well-known archipelagos.

The country of Japan is an archipelago. There are four main islands and many smaller ones.

CHAPTER TWO

CONTINENTAL ISLANDS

Continental islands are islands that were once connected to a continent and remain on the **continental shelf**. They are formed by movement of Earth's outer layer and changes in sea level. Wind and water can also form them.

Sometimes large continental islands have broken off from the main continental shelf. These are called microcontinents. Zealandia, near Australia, is a mostly underwater microcontinent. The only part above water is the island nation of New Zealand.

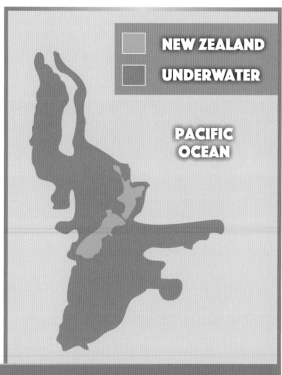

NEW ZEALAND

UNDERWATER

PACIFIC OCEAN

This map of Zealandia shows that 93 percent of the microcontinent is actually underwater.

Scientists believe that, millions of years ago, Earth had a single giant continent called Pangaea. Movement of Earth's outer layer broke Pangaea into several big pieces. These pieces slowly drifted and came to form the continents that we know today. When Pangaea was breaking up, there were also smaller pieces of land that broke off and became islands. Greenland is a continental island that formed this way.

Continental islands may also be formed by rising sea levels. During the Ice Age, much of Earth was covered in ice and the sea level was lower. As the ice began to melt, the sea level began to rise. Low-lying land flooded, and the areas left above the water became islands. The British Isles, once connected to the European **mainland**, were formed this way.

LOW TIDE

Mont-Saint-Michel is a famous tidal island in France. Here you can see the differences between low tide and high tide.

Another natural force that can create continental islands is erosion. Erosion is the wearing away of Earth's surface by wind or water. If a piece of land between two other pieces of land is worn away, an island may be created.

Tidal islands are a type of continental island also created by erosion. A tidal island forms when land between the mainland and an island is not completely eroded but is underwater at **high tide**.

HIGH TIDE

CHAPTER THREE

OCEANIC ISLANDS

Oceanic islands are formed by the eruptions of **volcanoes** on the ocean floor. Each eruption adds a new layer of rock to the volcano. An eruption is the explosion of gases, smoke, or hot liquid rock from a volcano. An underwater volcano may someday rise above the water, forming an island. Underwater volcanoes that have not yet broken the water's surface are called seamounts.

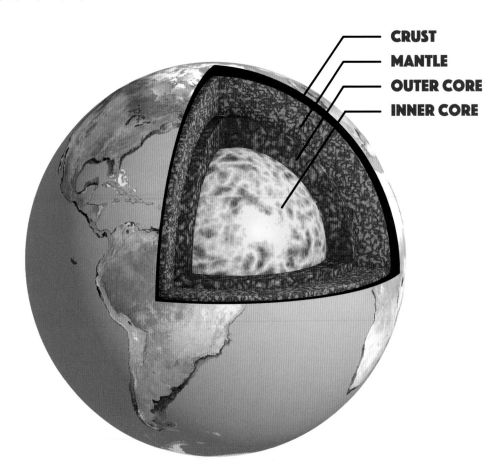

CRUST
MANTLE
OUTER CORE
INNER CORE

The oceanic islands of Japan were formed by volcanoes over the course of millions of years.

Earth has four main layers: the crust, mantle, outer **core**, and inner core. Volcanoes form when magma, or hot liquid rock, is able to move from the mantle up through Earth's crust. This usually happens where two plates, or pieces of Earth's crust and upper mantle meet. Plates "float" on the mantle and are always moving. Plate movement and magma flow can create different kinds of volcanoes.

Oceanic islands are created by different types of volcanoes. One type of volcano forms where subduction occurs. Subduction is when a heavier plate moves under the edge of a lighter plate. Magma is sometimes released, or let go, when this happens. The magma cools and hardens into a new layer of rock. With enough eruptions, a volcano can grow into an island.

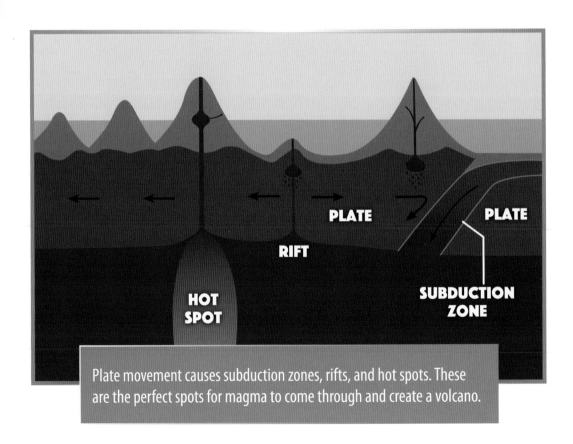

PLATE

PLATE

RIFT

HOT
SPOT

SUBDUCTION
ZONE

Plate movement causes subduction zones, rifts, and hot spots. These are the perfect spots for magma to come through and create a volcano.

In 1883, the volcanic island of Krakatoa in Indonesia erupted. Much of the island and the surrounding archipelago were destroyed.

Another type of volcano is created where two plates move away from each other. This movement is called a rift. When a rift occurs, magma from the mantle can move up through the crust and upper mantle, creating a volcano.

Oceanic islands can also be formed by hot spots. A hot spot is a place in the mantle where heat rises from deeper in the earth. The heat melts the nearby rock into magma. The magma is pushed up through the plate, forming a volcano. A hot spot doesn't move, but the plate above does. Over time, this can create a chain of islands.

CHAPTER FOUR

BARRIER ISLANDS

Narrow islands found along coasts are called barrier islands. These islands act as barriers, or walls, separating the mainland and the ocean. Barrier islands help protect coastlines from wind and waves.

An atoll is a coral reef that grows in a ring around an oceanic island. The reef continues to grow, even after the land sinks.

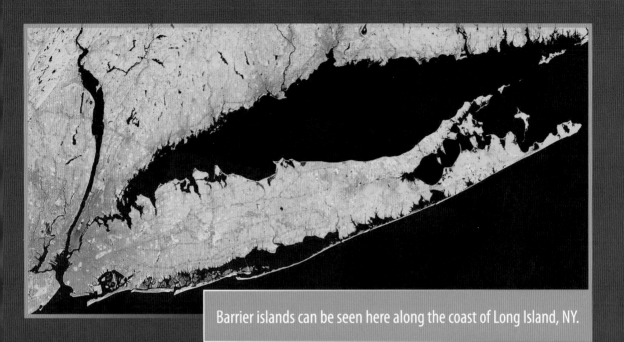
Barrier islands can be seen here along the coast of Long Island, NY.

Barrier islands made of coral are formed when reefs grow above the water level. Other barrier islands are made of **sediment**. Water often moves sand around, and sometimes the sand piles up. If it piles high enough, a barrier island can form. Islands in rivers are made this way. The currents that form barrier islands can also destroy them.

During the Ice Age, moving **glaciers** left piles of rock and soil along coastlines. Water from melting glaciers flooded the land, turning these sediment piles into barrier islands. The wind also left mounds of sand along coastlines. When melting glaciers flooded these areas, the sand mounds became barrier islands, too.

CHAPTER FIVE

ARTIFICIAL ISLANDS

Not all islands are formed by nature. Some islands are artificial, or made by humans. These islands provide more space for housing, farming, and even airports.

Artificial islands are sometimes built in special shapes. Palm Jebel Ali and The World are two artificial archipelagos in Dubai, United Arab Emirates.

Artificial islands are sometimes built in open water. Sand or rocks are brought in and piled up to form a brand-new island. **Engineers** in Dubai have built several islands by moving sand from the Persian Gulf closer to the shore. Sometimes other things are used. In 1998, a British man built Spiral Island off the coast of Mexico using more than 250,000 plastic bottles. Hurricane Emily destroyed the island in 2005, but another, Spiral Island II, has since been built.

Artificial islands may be enlaraged by removing the water from around an existing island. Engineers in 14th-century Mexico made more space to build their capital city, Tenochtitlán, by removing water from around an island in Lake Texcoco.

CLOSE-UP OF PALM JEBEL ALI

CHAPTER SIX

ARCHIPELAGOS

Groups of closely scattered islands are called archipelagos. Archipelagos are usually made up of oceanic islands, but they can also be found in lakes and rivers.

An island **arc** is an archipelago made of oceanic islands. Many island arcs form over a hot spot. Looking at the line of islands shows how a plate moved over the hot spot.

The Hawaiian Islands are a great example, as they continue to form this way. As the plate moves, the islands move away from the hot spot. When the hot spot is too far away to add to an island, the island begins to erode. The plate beneath the island cools and **shrinks**, and the island begins to sink back into the sea. Over a long period of time, an island can disappear completely.

Oahu is the third largest of the eight main Hawaiian Islands. A seamount called Loihi will someday become another island in this archipelago.

OAHU

HAWAIIAN
ISLANDS

LOIHI

Not all archipelagos are formed from volcanic activity. Many are formed from continental islands that were created after the Ice Age. Melting glaciers flooded the land and turned coastal mountain ranges into archipelagos.

The Malay Archipelago, located between the Indian and Pacific Oceans, was formed this way. It contains more than 25,000 islands and is the largest archipelago in the world. Some islands in the Malay Archipelago were once part of the Asian mainland. Water from melting glaciers flooded the area and separated these islands from the continent.

The Philippines is part of the Malay Archipelago. There are more than 7,000 Philippine Islands, but people only live on about 2,000 them. Around 5,000 of the islands don't even have names yet.

The Archipelago Sea in Finland has more than 50,000 islands, but many of them are very small. Tiny islands are called islets. Many of these islands were formed in a process called post-glacial rebound. This means that land once squashed by glaciers slowly returns to its original shape.

CHAPTER SEVEN

LOSING GROUND

Both nature and people can create islands, but they can also destroy them. Islands face natural erosion from water and wind every day. **Climate change** is making the problem worse.

The Marshall Islands is a nation made up of of 29 atolls and five small islands between Australia and Hawaii. Climate change has caused the sea level to rise, and the Marshall Islands see more flooding and higher tides each year. The amount of land available on the islands keeps getting smaller, and people are being forced to leave. Someday, the islands might be completely swallowed by the sea.

Other islands face the same kind of problems. Researchers recently discovered that five of the Solomon Islands have disappeared due to rising sea levels. Fortunately, scientists and engineers are hard at work studying climate change and its effects on islands.

GLOSSARY

arc (ARK) Something that is curved.

climate change (KLY-muht CHAYNJ) Change in Earth's weather caused by human activity.

continental shelf (kahn-tuh-NEHN-tuhl SHELF) The area of seabed around a large landmass where the sea is relatively shallow compared with the open ocean; part of the continental crust.

core (KOHR) The center of something.

engineer (en-juh-NEER) Someone who plans and builds machines, structures, and systems.

glacier (GLAY-shur) A large mass of ice that moves down a mountain or along a valley.

high tide (HY TYD) The time when ocean water is highest on the shore. The time when water is lowest on shore is called "low tide."

mainland (MAYN-land) An unbroken body of land making up the chief part of a country or continent.

sediment (SEH-dih-mehnt) Matter, such as stones and sand, that is carried onto land or into the water by wind, water, or land movement.

shrink (SHRINK) To become smaller in amount or size.

volcano (vahl-KAY-noh) An opening in Earth's surface through which hot, liquid rock sometimes flows.

INDEX

PRIMARY SOURCE LIST

Pages 8–9
(Page 8) Mont-Saint-Michel at low tide. Photo by Igor Plotnikov. From Shutterstock.com.
(Page 9) Mont-Saint-Michel at high tide. Photo by Kanuman. From Shutterstock.com.

Page 13
The eruption of Krakatoa in Indonesia in 1883. Lithograph by Parker & Coward, Britain. Plate 1 in *The Eruption of Krakatoa, and Subsequent Phenomena*. Report of the Krakatoa Committee of the Royal Society. Published by London, Trubner & Co., 1888.

Page 15
Barrier islands of Long Island, NY. Landsat satellite global mosaic image. From NASA/Jet Propulsion Laboratory.

WEBSITES

Due to the changing nature of Internet links, PowerKids Press has developed an online list of websites related to the subject of this book. This site is updated regularly. Please use this link to access the list: www.powerkidslinks.com/soes/isles